I0605769

NEWSMAKERS

# CAITLIN CLARK
## BASKETBALL STAR

BY LUKE HANLON

Cover image: Caitlin Clark began playing for the Indiana Fever in 2024.

An Imprint of Abdo Publishing
abdobooks.com

abdobooks.com

Published by Abdo Publishing, a division of ABDO, PO Box 398166, Minneapolis, Minnesota 55439. 

Printed in the United States of America, North Mankato, Minnesota.
102024
012025

Cover Photo: Jeff Dean/Getty Images Sport/Getty Images
Interior Photos: Keith Gillett/Icon Sportswire/Getty Images, 4–5, 19, 20, 37; Red Line Editorial, 7, 36; Matthew Holst/Getty Images Sport/Getty Images, 9, 22–23, 32–33, 43; Carmen Mandato/Getty Images Sport/Getty Images, 12–13; Mitchell Layton/Getty Images Sport/Getty Images, 14; Shutterstock Images, 17; G. Fiume/Getty Images Sport/Getty Images, 25, 45; David Berding/Getty Images Sport/Getty Images, 27; Tyler Schank/C. Morgan Engel/NCAA Photos/Getty Images, 28; Ben Solomon/NCAA Photos/Getty Images, 30; State Farm, 34; Elsa/Getty Images Sport/Getty Images, 40

Editor: Katharine Hale
Series Designer: Marley Richmond

**Library of Congress Control Number: 2024938345**

**Publisher's Cataloging-in-Publication Data**

Names: Hanlon, Luke, author.
Title: Caitlin Clark: basketball star / by Luke Hanlon
Other title: basketball star
Description: Minneapolis, Minnesota: ABDO Publishing, 2025 | Series: Newsmakers | Includes online resources and index.
Identifiers: ISBN 9781098295684 (lib. bdg.) | ISBN 9798384916680 (ebook)
Subjects: LCSH: Clark, Caitlin, 2002---Juvenile literature. | WNBA superstars--Biography--Juvenile literature. | Women basketball players--Biography--Juvenile literature. | Indiana Fever (Basketball team)--Juvenile literature. | Professional athletes--Biography--Juvenile literature. | Basketball--Juvenile literature.
Classification: DDC 796.323092--dc23

# CONTENTS

**CHAPTER ONE**
**Record Breaker** ........ 4

**CHAPTER TWO**
**Immediate Success** ........ 12

**CHAPTER THREE**
**Household Name** ........ 22

**CHAPTER FOUR**
**Changing the Game** ........ 32

**Important Dates** ........ 42

**Stop and Think** ........ 44

**Glossary** ........ 46

**Online Resources** ........ 47

**Learn More** ........ 47

**Index** ........ 48

**About the Author** ........ 48

IOWA
22

CHAPTER ONE

# RECORD BREAKER

Caitlin Clark buried a jump shot and picked up three points for her team. Now they were leading 5–2. Clark had been thrilling fans in Iowa City, Iowa, and arenas across the country for four years. She had made hundreds of three-pointers in her career. But tonight was special. Coming into the game on February 15, 2024, Clark needed eight points to break the National Collegiate Athletic Association (NCAA) women's basketball scoring record.

Caitlin Clark is known for her impressive three-point shots.

The Iowa Hawkeyes were playing against the University of Michigan. Clark started the game off hot, scoring 5 points in the game's opening 42 seconds.

Soon after, Hawkeye guard Gabbie Marshall rebounded a missed Michigan shot. She passed to Clark. Clark crossed halfcourt. After one more dribble, she gathered for a shot 35 feet (11 m) away from the basket. Nothing but net! The Iowa fans erupted. Clark had now scored 3,528 points during her college career, more than any other woman in NCAA history. Iowa coach Lisa Bluder took a time-out so the crowd could show Clark even more love.

Clark went on to score 49 points in the win against Michigan. No Iowa player had ever scored that many points in a game. And Clark had more records in sight before the end of her senior season.

## HOMETOWN HERO

Caitlin Clark was born on January 22, 2002, in West Des Moines, Iowa. The Clark household

## TOP NCAA SCORERS

| | NAME | TEAM | POINTS | FINAL SEASON |
|---|---|---|---|---|
| 1 | Caitlin Clark | Iowa | 3,951 | 2024 |
| 2 | Pete Maravich | LSU | 3,667 | 1970 |
| 3 | Antoine Davis | Detroit Mercy | 3,664 | 2023 |
| 4 | Kelsey Plum | Washington | 3,527 | 2017 |
| 5 | Dyaisha Fair | Buffalo/ Syracuse | 3,403 | 2024 |
| 6 | Kelsey Mitchell | Ohio State | 3,402 | 2018 |
| 7 | Jackie Stiles | Missouri State | 3,393 | 2001 |
| 8 | Brittney Griner | Baylor | 3,283 | 2013 |
| 9 | Freeman Williams | Portland State | 3,249 | 1978 |
| 10 | Chris Clemons | Campbell | 3,225 | 2019 |

Clark broke Kelsey Plum's NCAA scoring record, which had stood since 2017. Clark finished her college career with 3,951 points. This table lists the top 10 all-time leading scorers in NCAA women's and men's basketball. What do you notice about the point differences over time?

embraced competition. Caitlin's father, Brent, had played basketball and baseball at Simpson College in Indianola, Iowa. Caitlin's older brother, Blake, played football at Iowa State University (ISU) in Ames. And her younger brother, Colin, also played basketball.

## LONG-RANGE SHOOTER

The deep three that Caitlin Clark hit to set the NCAA career scoring record was nothing new to her. The three-point line is 22 feet and 1.75 inches away from the basket. But Clark routinely made shots from beyond 25 feet. To honor her record-breaking basket, Iowa marked the spot on the court where she made the shot. The logo featured Clark's name and jersey number.

When Caitlin wasn't competing against her brothers, she was playing against other boys. There weren't many opportunities for girls to play basketball, so Caitlin had to play on boys' leagues. When Caitlin was five, there was a game where a much bigger boy guarded her. He played rough, using his size to intimidate her. Caitlin was frustrated. Brent took Caitlin out of the game. She composed herself on the bench. Once she re-entered the game, she went right after the boy who guarded her, blocked him, and stood over him when he fell. She wasn't going to be intimidated anymore.

Clark's family joined her for Senior Day at her final regular-season game in 2024.

At 13, Caitlin began playing on the varsity team at Dowling Catholic High School. She competed against girls who were older than she was. But she still stood out. University of Iowa assistant coach Jan Jensen went to watch Caitlin play as an eighth grader. Jensen said it took less than a minute to realize Caitlin's skills were special.

Clark played for Dowling Catholic for four seasons. By her sophomore year, she was one of the top recruits in the country. Caitlin showcased great shooting and passing skills. As a junior, she averaged 32.6 points per game and won the Iowa Gatorade Player of the

## HIGH SCHOOL SUPERSTAR

One of Caitlin's high school games stood out more than others. On February 4, 2019, she started out hot against Mason City High School. In the first quarter, Caitlin made six three-pointers. Multiple Mason City defenders swarmed Caitlin. But there was nothing they could do. She finished the game with a state record of 13 three-pointers. And she scored 60 points, just one point away from tying the state record for the most points in a girls' high school basketball game. After the game, Mason City students lined up to get Caitlin's autograph.

Year Award. Caitlin won that award again her senior year, when she increased her points-per-game average to 33.4.

Almost every top women's college basketball team wanted Caitlin. With her choice of the top programs, she narrowed her decision to the University of Iowa, ISU, and the University of Notre Dame. Before the start of her senior season in 2019, Caitlin announced that she would play for the University of Iowa Hawkeyes.

# STRAIGHT TO THE SOURCE

During Clark's career at Iowa, a lot of people compared her to National Basketball Association (NBA) Golden State Warriors superstar Steph Curry. Like Clark, Curry dominated games with his long-range threes. Curry said comparing her to him takes away from how good Clark is:

> *I've been watching from afar and understanding just how much of a power she is out there on the court. The cool part is the way that she plays, and her range, and the level of difficulty on her shots is obviously a very close comparison to the way that I play. . . . But I think it almost robs her of the rest of her game because she's such a good floor [general], she has her overall floor game. She's racking up close to triple-doubles every night. Her shooting ability is her superpower, but the rest of her game is as polished as that, and so this is must-see TV.*

Source: Isabel Gonzales. "Warriors' Stephen Curry Shares Thoughts on Caitlin Clark Comparisons, Says Iowa Star Is 'Must-See TV.'" *CBS Sports*, 12 Mar. 2024, cbssports.com. Accessed 25 Jun. 2024.

## WHAT'S THE BIG IDEA?

Read Curry's quote carefully. What is the main point he's trying to make? Explain how that idea is supported by details.

NCAA
B1G
Iowa
22
BLM
5

CHAPTER TWO

# IMMEDIATE SUCCESS

Due to Clark's skills in high school, Hawkeye fans expected greatness right away. That's a lot of pressure to put on an 18-year-old. But Clark was not overwhelmed.

Coming into the 2020–21 season, the Hawkeyes had lost three out of their five starting players from the previous year. Clark slotted right into the starting lineup on November 25, 2020, when she made her college debut against the University of

**Star freshmen Caitlin Clark and Paige Bueckers, *right*, faced off in the 2021 NCAA tournament.**

**Clark was a team player, setting records in assists as well as points.**

Northern Iowa. On the first offensive possession of the game for Iowa, Clark showcased her aggressiveness by driving toward the basket to earn two free throws. She made them both and scored her first college points. She kept scoring after that, finishing the game with 27 points and a victory for Iowa.

Clark's transition from high school to college basketball looked seamless. She had no trouble scoring against top competitors. And she displayed offensive skills beyond just shooting. In her sixth career game, she recorded a triple-double of 13 points, 13 rebounds, and 10 assists. A triple-double is when a player records ten or more of three different stats. Those stats are points, rebounds, assists, steals, and blocks.

## FABULOUS FRESHMAN

Clark starting setting women's college basketball records during her first season. Her 26.6 points per game were the highest scoring average by a freshman in 35 years. Clark scored 30 or more points in 12 different games in the 2020–21 season. No freshman had done that in 20 years. She became only the second freshman to lead the country in scoring. Ohio State's Kelsey Mitchell first did that in the 2015–16 season with an average of 24.9 points per game.

Stellar performances became a regular occurrence for Clark during that first season. No player in the country scored as many points as she did that year, and only two players recorded more assists per game. Clark continued to play well in the NCAA tournament. The tournament starts with 68 teams. As losing teams are eliminated, the 16 remaining teams are called the Sweet 16. The final eight teams are the Elite Eight, and the winners become the Final Four. To win the tournament, a team needs to win six games in a row.

Clark scored 35 points to help Iowa upset the University of Kentucky in the second round. Iowa then faced the University of Connecticut (UConn) in the Sweet 16. Connecticut freshman Paige Bueckers came into college as the top-ranked high-school player in the country. She and the Huskies proved to be too much for the Hawkeyes, as Connecticut won 92–72.

## SOPHOMORE SURGE

Before Clark started her sophomore year, she represented the United States at the 2021 Under-19 Women's Basketball World Cup. The tournament featured the best players from around the world.

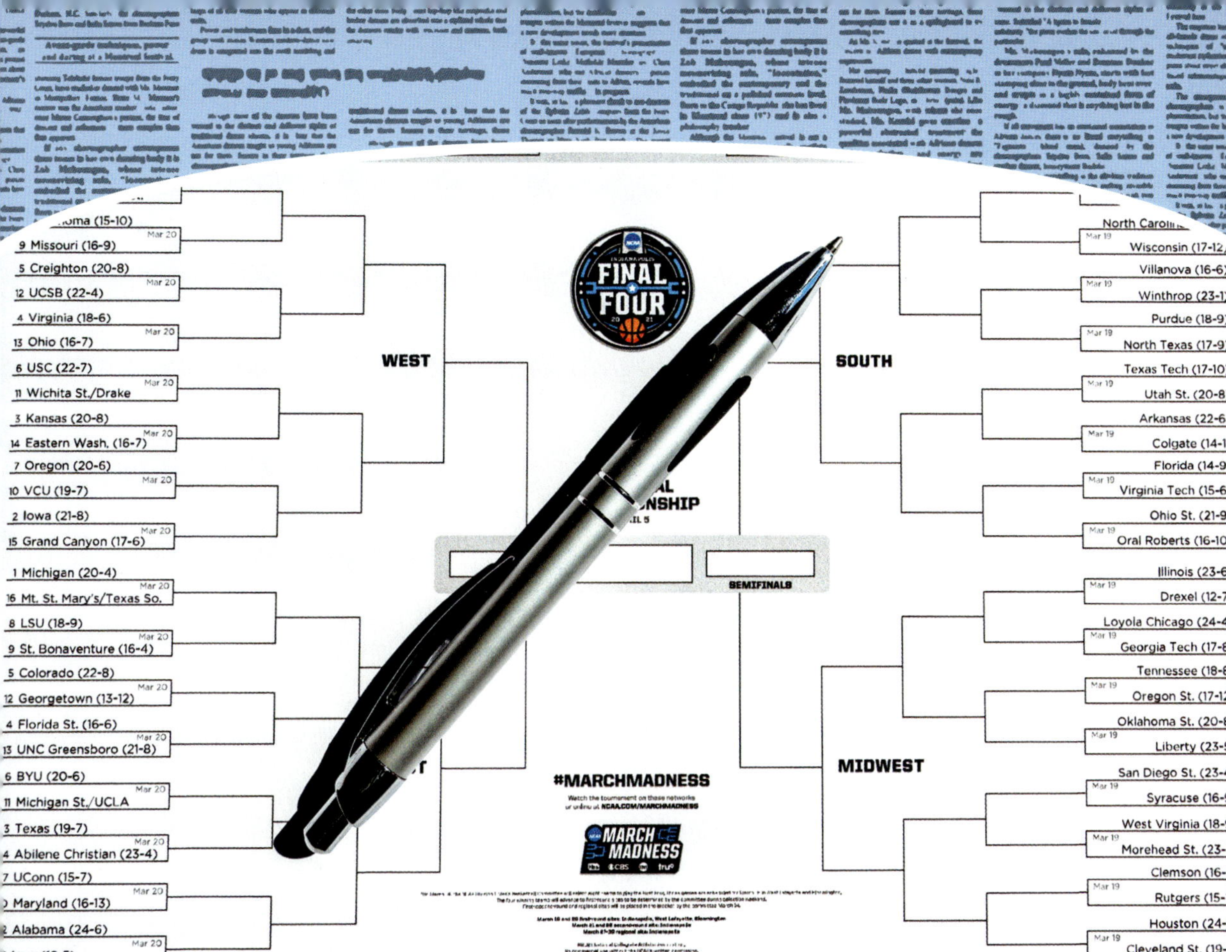


**The NCAA tournament is set up in brackets, with teams being eliminated after each lost game. People can participate in March Madness by filling out their own brackets.**

Clark led the United States to a perfect 7–0 record to win the gold medal on August 15. She earned Most Valuable Player (MVP) honors for her performance.

Clark carried that momentum into the college season. She continued to show off a full offensive game, tallying five triple-doubles in the 2021–22 season.

## FEEDING FAMILIES

Caitlin Clark has always tried to give back to her community. After her sophomore season, Clark partnered with the Coralville Community Food Pantry near Iowa City. This charity helps families that struggle to afford food. Clark urged Iowa fans to donate $22 to the food pantry in honor of her jersey number. Fans who donated money received a Clark basketball card. They were also entered into a drawing to win a signed Clark jersey. The food pantry received more than $100,000 in donations.

Her scoring improved as well. That January, she scored a career-high 44 points in a win against the University of Evansville. A month later, Clark scored 46 points against the University of Michigan.

As in her freshman year, Clark once again finished as the country's leading scorer. For her outstanding conference play throughout the season, Clark won the Big Ten Player of the Year Award. She then continued to dominate in the Big Ten Tournament. In the semifinals against the University of

Clark and the Hawkeyes beat the Illinois State Redbirds 98–58 in the first round of the 2022 NCAA tournament.

Nebraska, Clark scored from all over the floor, putting up 41 points. The next day, Iowa beat the University of Indiana to secure the Big Ten title.

Many people expected the Hawkeyes to make a deep run in the NCAA tournament. Playing in front of a home crowd, Iowa easily beat Illinois State University in the opening round. The Hawkeyes then hosted Creighton University in the second round. Creighton's best player, Lauren Jensen, had transferred from Iowa after not playing much the year before. She returned to Iowa City with a point to prove. With 15 seconds left, Jensen hit a three to put Creighton up by one. On the

CREIGHTON
15
CREIGHT
13
HOSTED BY

next possession, Clark drove hard to the hoop. But her layup attempt clanked off the rim. Creighton held on to pull off the upset.

Clark struggled in the losing game. She made only 4 of the 19 shots she took. Two years after the game, Clark said this was the lowest point of her career. But it only fueled her competitive edge. She vowed to come back stronger for her junior year.

## EXPLORE ONLINE

Chapter Two discusses Caitlin Clark's early career at the University of Iowa. After the 2020–21 season, the Women's Basketball Coaches Association (WBCA) announced Paige Bueckers and Caitlin Clark as the NCAA Division I Co-Freshmen of the Year. Visit the website below to read the WBCA's press release about the award. What new information did you learn?

### 2021 WBCA NCAA DIVISION I CO-FRESHMEN OF THE YEAR

abdocorelibrary.com/caitlin-clark

Clark and the Hawkeyes fell short to Creighton in the second round of the 2022 NCAA tournament.

77
99

CHAPTER THREE

# HOUSEHOLD NAME

After her sophomore season, Clark became one of the most popular players in college basketball. Fans loved watching her launch long step-back threes. Her offensive skills reminded a lot of basketball fans of Steph Curry, one of the most popular players in the National Basketball Association (NBA). Television networks started to notice the excitement surrounding Clark. As a result, Iowa had 18 games televised during the 2022–23 season. That included two games

Clark interacted with fans after playing an exhibition game at Kinnick Stadium.

broadcast on FOX, one of the most-watched networks. FOX had never aired a Big Ten women's basketball game before. But Clark changed that.

Clark made the most of playing in front of a wider TV audience. On January 7, 2023, FOX aired Iowa's trip to Michigan to take on the Wolverines. Michigan was one of the best teams in the Big Ten. Clark wasn't fazed, as she scored 28 points and grabbed 8 rebounds to stun Michigan fans and lead Iowa to a 94–85 win.

Three weeks later, FOX broadcast Iowa's home game against Nebraska. This time, Iowa started out slow. The Hawkeyes didn't score a point in the game's first four minutes. With the team down 8–0, Clark hit a three to put Iowa on the board. The floodgates opened from there. Through Clark's pinpoint shooting and crisp passing, the Hawkeyes took control of the game. Clark finished with 33 points, 12 rebounds, and 9 assists to cap off another great performance.

Clark didn't hog the ball from her teammates. She tallied at least 8 assists in 11 straight games

**Clark faced Cotie McMahon, *right*, and the Ohio State Buckeyes on January 23, 2023.**

starting in early January 2023. That included a 15-assist performance at Ohio State University to hand the Buckeyes their first loss of the season. For the second season in a row, Clark led the country in assists per game.

Clark continued her hot streak into the Big Ten Tournament. Thousands of fans flocked to Minneapolis,

## CLUTCH SHOT

Iowa and Indiana were two of the top Big Ten teams during the 2022–23 season. On February 9, Indiana beat Iowa 87–78. The two teams met again two weeks later in Iowa City. With 1.5 seconds left, Indiana led the game 85–83. Iowa had the ball and drew up a play for Clark. Coming off a screen, she received the ball and heaved it toward the basket while fading to her right. The shot went in after the buzzer sounded, allowing Iowa to pull off a dramatic win.

Minnesota, to see her play. For the first time in the tournament's history, the event completely sold out. Clark made sure to give the spectators their money's worth. She helped the Hawkeyes win their first two games. Facing Ohio State in the title game, Clark played one of the best games of her career. She ran every aspect of the Iowa offense, scoring 30 points and racking up 17 assists. She added 10 rebounds to become the first player ever to record a triple-double in a Big Ten championship game. Clark's performance secured another Big Ten title for Iowa.

The Hawkeyes bested the Buckeyes in the 2023 Big Ten championship.

## MARCH MADNESS

Iowa entered the 2023 NCAA tournament with big expectations. Unlike in the previous year, the Hawkeyes avoided an upset in the second round. As Iowa progressed in the tournament, Clark stepped up her game. In the Sweet 16, she scored 31 points and tallied 8 assists to advance past the University of Colorado. Clark then delivered a masterful performance in the Elite Eight, as she made 8 three-pointers and scored

**Clark celebrated with coach Lisa Bluder, *front right*, and her teammates after earning a spot in the Final Four of the 2023 NCAA tournament.**

41 points. She added 12 assists and 10 rebounds to lift the Hawkeyes to victory and send them to the Final Four for the first time in 30 years.

The University of South Carolina stood in Iowa's way of making the championship game. The Gamecocks came into the matchup on March 31 with an undefeated record. Most people expected them to roll past the Hawkeyes. But Iowa had a plan. The Gamecocks dominated near the basket. But they didn't hit many three-pointers. Iowa players stayed close to the basket on defense and left South Carolina players open to shoot three-pointers.

Iowa's plan worked. The Gamecocks made only 4 of the 20 threes they attempted. Meanwhile, Clark made 5 three-pointers and scored 41 points overall. Her offensive outburst earned Iowa a chance to play for the national championship.

The Hawkeyes faced Louisiana State University (LSU) in the title game. The Tigers had a talented team, including star forward

## WADE TROPHY

**Before the Final Four, the Women's Basketball Coaches Association (WBCA) named Clark the winner of the Wade Trophy. That trophy is awarded to the best women's college basketball player in the country each year. While Clark said she doesn't play basketball for individual awards, she considered winning the award a huge honor.**

**The Hawkeyes fought hard but fell short to Angel Reese, *center*, and the LSU Tigers in the title game of the 2023 NCAA tournament.**

Angel Reese. Fans couldn't wait to see Clark and Reese face each other. In fact, 9.9 million people watched the championship game. It became the most-watched women's college basketball game of all time.

Clark stepped up to the challenge in the title game. She buried 8 three-pointers and finished with a game-high 30 points. However, the Hawkeyes couldn't stop Reese and her teammates. LSU ran away with a 102–85 win to claim the championship.

# STRAIGHT TO THE SOURCE

Caitlin Clark is a fierce competitor who plays with a lot of emotion. This can include taunting and trash talk. After winning the 2023 national championship game, Angel Reese taunted Clark using a gesture Clark had used previously. Iowa fans heavily criticized Reese, especially on social media. Clark defended Reese:

> *I think men have always had trash talk. I think that's what it's always been. . . . I'm just lucky enough that I get to play this game and have emotion and wear it on my sleeves. So does everybody else. That should never be torn down. That should never be criticized because I believe that's what makes this game so fun. That's what draws people to this game. That's what draws it to the pro level, to the college level, to the high school level.*

Source: Austin Nivison. "Caitlin Clark Says LSU's Angel Reese 'Should Never Be Criticized' for Taunting Gestures on Court." *CBS Sports*, 4 Apr. 2023, cbssports.com. Accessed 25 Jun. 2024.

## CHANGING MINDS

In this quote, Clark defends trash talking during games. Take a position on taunting in basketball, and then imagine that your best friend has the opposite opinion. Write a short essay trying to change your friend's mind. Make sure you explain your opinion. Include facts and details to support your points.

KINNICK STADIUM
IOWA

CHAPTER FOUR

# CHANGING THE GAME

Caitlin Clark's senior year became all about shattering records. In fact, Clark helped break a record before Iowa's season officially began. On October 15, 2023, Iowa played in an exhibition game against DePaul University. But it didn't take place in Carver-Hawkeye Arena, Iowa's basketball arena. Instead, the two teams played outdoors at Kinnick Stadium, where Iowa's football team plays. A crowd of 55,646 fans went to the game, making

**The Hawkeyes played a record-breaking exhibition game at Kinnick Stadium in 2023.**

**Clark was the first college athlete signed by insurance company State Farm. She appeared in a national commercial for State Farm and in ads for other companies.**

it the highest-attended women's college basketball game ever.

During Clark's senior year, her popularity led to endorsement deals with major brands such as Nike and Gatorade. In the past, student-athletes were not allowed to make money from their name, image, and likeness. Rules changed in 2021, allowing Clark to make an estimated $3.1 million on endorsement deals.

Clark never let the off-the-court attention affect her performance. For the fourth straight year, she increased her number of points and assists per game. And for the second time in her career, she led the country in both of those stats. With all that scoring, Clark climbed up the list of the highest-scoring players in college basketball history. On February 15, 2024, Clark passed Washington legend Kelsey Plum for the most points in NCAA women's basketball history.

The NCAA began holding championships for women's basketball in 1982. Before then, the Association for Intercollegiate Athletics for Women ran women's college basketball. From 1977 to 1981, Lynette Woodard scored 3,649 points while playing for the University of Kansas. No one had scored that many points since the NCAA took over.

On February 28, 2024, Iowa played the University of Minnesota. Coming into the game, Clark needed 33 points to break Woodard's record. She came out firing, scoring Iowa's first 15 points of the game. By the middle of the fourth quarter, Clark had scored 30 points. She then drained her eighth three-pointer of the game to officially become the highest scorer in women's college basketball history.

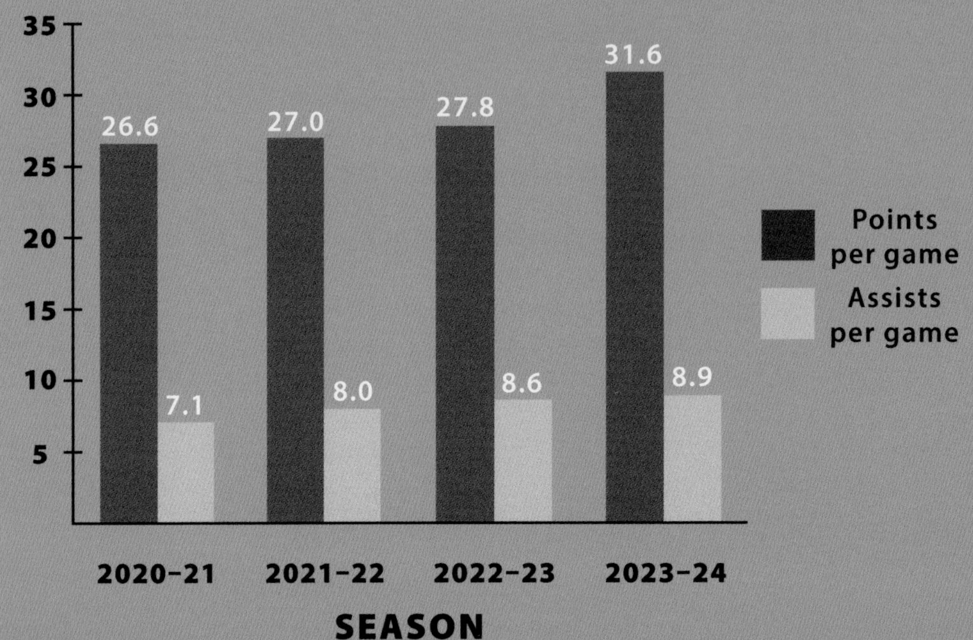


Each year at Iowa, Clark increased her average points per game and assists per game, demonstrating what made her such a complete offensive superstar. How do you think she was able to improve her stats each season?

Only one career scoring record remained. No college basketball player had ever scored more than LSU legend Pete Maravich. From 1967 to 1970, he racked up 3,667 points. Ahead of her final regular-season home game, Clark needed 18 points to pass Maravich. On March 3, she made two free throws right before halftime to break Maravich's record.

Clark and teammate Hannah Stuelke defend during Clark's final regular-season game on March 3, 2024.

Clark was now the highest scorer college basketball had ever seen.

## ONE LAST RUN

Before the start of the 2024 Big Ten Tournament, Clark announced that she would be entering the Women's National Basketball Association (WNBA) Draft after the season. Knowing this would be her last run with Iowa, she left everything on the court. Clark led the Hawkeyes to their third-straight Big Ten Tournament championship. She then carried Iowa back to the Elite Eight in the NCAA tournament, where a familiar opponent was waiting for them. Defending champions LSU and Angel Reese stood in Iowa's way of making back-to-back Final Fours.

Both teams started out hot, with Reese and Clark trading buckets throughout the first half. With the score tied 45–45 at halftime, Clark began to take over in the second half. No defensive strategy LSU used could slow Clark down. She recorded 41 points and 12 assists to get revenge against LSU and lead Iowa back to the Final Four.

Iowa faced the UConn Huskies in the Final Four. Paige Bueckers and the Huskies had eliminated Iowa in the tournament

## HOT TICKET

Going to Carver-Hawkeye Arena became an expensive outing during the 2023–24 season. People wanted to see Clark play in person. Tickets to an Iowa home game resold for an average price of $180 that year. The prices went up once Clark started breaking records. Before her final regular-season home game, the average resale ticket price jumped to approximately $550. The most expensive ticket for that game sold for $1,001.

three years prior. They were ready for the challenge. UConn's defense forced Clark into tough shots throughout the game. Iowa trailed for most of the game, but Clark made three three-pointers in the second half to help send the Hawkeyes to the championship.

## ALL EYES ON CAITLIN

On April 2, 2023, just under ten million people watched the national championship game between Iowa and LSU. That became the most-watched women's college basketball game ever. When the teams faced off again in the 2024 Elite Eight, the game averaged 12.3 million viewers. Then when Iowa played UConn in the Final Four, 14.2 million people watched. Finally, 18.7 million people tuned in when South Carolina won the national championship against Iowa. No college or professional basketball game had drawn that many viewers since 2019.

On April 7, 2024, Clark's final game for Iowa came against another team from her past. Just as in 2023, South Carolina entered the matchup with an undefeated record. Clark came in ready to pull off another upset.

Clark continues to impress in the WNBA. The Indiana Fever often draws record-breaking crowds, with some games needing to move to larger arenas.

She made a three-pointer to give Iowa an early lead. Clark finished the first quarter with 18 points.

But South Carolina fought back. The Gamecocks took control and went on to finish their undefeated season with an 87–75 win. Although Clark lost her final college game, South Carolina head coach Dawn Staley thanked her for the impact she had made on the sport. She said Clark was one of the greatest women's college basketball players of all time and that she would increase the popularity of the WNBA.

Just a week later, on April 15, the Indiana Fever selected Clark with the top pick in the WNBA Draft.

Playing against tougher competition, Clark struggled to put up the stats she did in college. The Fever lost eight out of their first nine games. But Clark quickly adjusted to the WNBA. She scored 30 points in her eighth career game. Clark also racked up assists when defenses wouldn't let her score herself. Fans voted Clark into the WNBA All-Star Game, placing her among the best players in the league. A record-breaking 3.44 million people tuned in to see Clark, Reese, and the other All Stars win against the US Olympic team on July 20. The future looked bright for one of basketball's most exciting players.

## FURTHER EVIDENCE

**Chapter Four talks about the start of Caitlin Clark's WNBA career. What was one of the main points? This website shows Clark's stats in the WNBA. Find a stat to support the main point of this chapter.**

### WNBA STATS: CAITLIN CLARK

**abdocorelibrary.com/caitlin-clark**

# IMPORTANT DATES

**January 22, 2002**
Caitlin Clark is born in West Des Moines, Iowa.

**February 4, 2019**
Caitlin scores 60 points in a game for Dowling Catholic High School, falling one point short of tying the state record for most points in a girls' high school basketball game.

**November 25, 2020**
Clark scores 27 points in her first game for Iowa, a win against the University of Northern Iowa.

**August 15, 2021**
Clark is named the MVP of the Under-19 Women's Basketball World Cup after she helped the United States win gold.

**March 31, 2023**
Behind Clark's 41 points, Iowa hands South Carolina its first loss of the season and advances the Hawkeyes to their first national title game in school history.

**March 3, 2024**
Clark passes Pete Maravich to become the all-time points leader in college basketball history.

**April 7, 2024**
In her final college game, Clark scores 18 points in the first quarter of the national championship game against South Carolina. However, the Gamecocks go on to win the game 87–75.

**April 15, 2024**
The Indiana Fever select Clark with the top pick in the 2024 WNBA Draft.

# STOP AND THINK

## Take a Stand

When Caitlin Clark broke many records during her senior year, fans started debating whether she was the best women's college basketball player ever. Some said her scoring records proved her greatness. Others said Clark not winning a championship meant there were other players who were better. Do you think Clark is the greatest women's college basketball player of all time? Why or why not?

## Tell the Tale

Chapter Two of this book discusses Caitlin Clark losing to Creighton early in the 2022 NCAA tournament. Imagine you are responding to a disappointing loss. Write 200 words about what it's like to bounce back after a tough loss. What do you think it would take to come back stronger after losing?

## Dig Deeper

After reading this book, what questions do you still have about Caitlin Clark? With an adult's help, find a few reliable

sources that can help you answer your questions. Write a paragraph about what you learned.

## Another View

This book talks about Caitlin Clark and Angel Reese playing with emotion on the court and supporting one another off the court. As you know, every source is different. Ask a librarian or another adult to help you find a second source about their relationship. Write a short essay comparing and contrasting the new source's point of view with that of this book's author. What is the point of view of each author? How are they similar and why? How are they different and why?

# GLOSSARY

**conference**
a group of schools that join together to create a league for their sports teams

**draft**
a system that allows teams to hire new players coming into a league

**exhibition**
a game that doesn't count in the standings

**floor general**
a player, usually a point guard, who runs a team's offense and sets up their teammates to score

**layup**
a shot made from close to the basket

**recruit**
a high school player capable of playing college sports

**screen**
when an offensive player legally blocks a defender to open up a teammate for a shot or a pass

**step-back**
a jump shot in which a player moves backward to create space to shoot

**upset**
an unexpected victory by a supposedly weaker team or player

**varsity**
the top level of high school sports

# ONLINE RESOURCES

To learn more about Caitlin Clark, visit our free resource websites below.

Visit **abdocorelibrary.com** or scan this QR code for free Common Core resources for teachers and students, including vetted activities, multimedia, and booklinks, for deeper subject comprehension.

Visit **abdobooklinks.com** or scan this QR code for free additional online weblinks for further learning. These links are routinely monitored and updated to provide the most current information available.

# LEARN MORE

Davidson, Keith B. *WNBA*. Crabtree, 2022.

Flynn, Brendan. *Girls' Basketball*. Abdo, 2022.

Hanlon, Luke. *Everything Basketball*. Abdo, 2025.

# INDEX

Big Ten Tournament, 18–19, 25–26, 37
Bluder, Lisa, 6
Bueckers, Paige, 16, 21, 38–39

college career, 13–40
Creighton, 19–21
Curry, Steph, 11, 23

Dowling Catholic High School, 9–10

family, 6–8

Indiana Fever, 40–41
Iowa City, Iowa, 5, 18, 19, 26
ISU, 7, 10

Jensen, Jan, 9
Jensen, Lauren, 19

LSU, 7, 29–30, 31, 36, 38, 39

Maravich, Pete, 7, 36
Marshall, Gabbie, 6
Mitchell, Kelsey, 7, 15

NCAA tournament, 16, 19–21, 27–30, 31, 37–40

Ohio State, 7, 15, 25, 26

Plum, Kelsey, 7, 35

records, 5–6, 7, 8, 10, 15, 33–34, 35–37, 38, 41
Reese, Angel, 29–30, 31, 38, 41

Staley, Dawn, 40

UConn, 16, 38–39
University of Michigan, 6, 18, 24
University of South Carolina, 28–29, 39–40

WNBA, 37, 40–41
Women's Basketball World Cup, 16–17
Woodard, Lynette, 35

## About the Author

Luke Hanlon is a sportswriter and editor based in Minneapolis, Minnesota. He's written dozens of nonfiction sports books for kids and spends a lot of his free time watching his favorite Minnesota sports teams.